ACKN

I want to thank my family and friends for their contributions over my lifetime experiences.

To Yolanda, my college sweetheart and soul mate who I have been happily married to for over 20 years and guides my heart.

My two brothers; Roberto and Raphael, my two sons; Paolo and Piero and most importantly my Mother and Father who helped to shape me to be the man I am today.

Most people look for mentors, heroes, and leaders to emulate. I have been lucky most of my life.

My Father, Romano Intrieri, taught me quite a bit with very few words. He was one that did what was right and never apologized for it.

My Mother, Lucia is my heart and the one that taught me to lead with compassion. I thank them ALL for all I have and am today.

1

CHAPTERS

WHERE THE REAL CHESS GAME IS PLAYED

In an increasingly complex world, can three-dimensional thinking eliminate the threat of unintended consequences for today's corporate executives?

As we start I have a confession to make: I love Star Trek. What a great television program and such a lasting memory of my childhood. For anyone, like myself, who grew up dreaming of serving on the Starship Enterprise under the brave command of Captain Kirk and the cool logic of Mr. Spock, there was one game we wanted to play: three dimensional chess. From the earliest episodes, we saw Mr. Spock pondering his next move on what

 looked at the time to be a super-futuristic multi-level chessboard. I dreamed of playing it from the first moment I saw it. What were the rules? The complexity must be unbearable? Could I ever defeat Mr. Spock? It was one of the endearing images of my childhood as I went to school and talked about the previous episode with my friends. We would think in our minds about how we could ever come up with such a game and how we would be the masters at it. Obviously technology wasn't able to produce such a game in the days of my youth but it never stopped me from dreaming about it. So, yes, I was one of those rare children who dreamed about being Mr. Spock.

Years later, Star Trek fans invented a three dimensional chessboard and rules for the game. I never purchased it. My childhood dreams had already morphed into grown-up ambition. Although I have always had a soft spot in my heart for Star Trek I had left the days of buying

3

memorabilia behind me and moved on to more grown up matters. But the thought never really went away.

Recently, though, as I became aware that a new Star Trek movie is due for release in May this year, I thought back again to my childhood and the three-dimensional chessboard. All those memories came flooding back and I thought about the hours I would spend contemplating that chessboard and Mr. Spock. Suddenly, I had a realization... I've been playing this game every day of my professional career. The three-dimensional chessboard never really went away. Actually, it has been a key source of management strength since my days as a mid-level executive. I have been going about my daily business in a way that resembles the three-dimensional chessboard. Every move I made had consequences for each and every future move I could make. I hadn't thought about it in this way before but I was involved in a long-term chess game that had been my career. I was able to think about what my next move would mean to those around me. I was playing there dimensional chess in a way that made me a better manager, that made me more considerate of those people I worked with and enabled me to think several moves ahead.

I realized that understanding the consequences; both intended and unintended, of your decisions at the strategic, tactical and operational levels is one of the primary drivers of success for any manager in any organization. The moves you make, the decisions you enact will impact on everyone else in your organization at many different levels. Take, for example a decision to roll out a new product. It is something that many companies undertake every single year. But just saying we are going to roll out a new product takes more than just making that decision. The product needs to be developed and tested. Your customers have to be informed through advertising and marketing that you have a new product available. Your shareholders need to understand what this will do differently for them in terms of sales and profits. Your own sales team needs to be trained on the new product, its features and how to sell it. The social media team needs to know the potential enquiries they will receive about it and know how to respond. The recruitment team may need to hire more sales people to get this new product out there. And the list goes on. What seemed like a simple decision to launch a new product has implications on many levels at many different parts of the business. Understanding how your strategic moves will impact operations two levels down from your command is not a simple task. You have to take the time to learn, in real terms, how your decisions impact the entire organization. It requires thinking in three dimensions... much like Mr. Spock staring at the chessboard on the Starship Enterprise. Now you can see how every single decision you make has implications that you may not have been able to conceive at the time of making that decision.

I am not asking you to think of your moves as though they were on a three-dimensional chessboard. That might just fry your brain but what I am suggesting is that by using the power of the techniques I will show you in this book you can be a more thoughtful leader of people. They by considering the consequences of all of your actions you will be able to make decision that work for both the organization you are working in and the others that work there too. Everyone has a right to feel happy and valued at work. That is a basic human right that changes the average worker from someone who just turns up and punches in to someone that contributes and makes a difference. Every company wants a team that is full of the latter, and as few of the former as possible - a team of motivated individuals that contribute to the success of the company. But in large organizations particularly this can be difficult to achieve. There can be so many levels and hierarchies that some people feel unwanted or simply left behind when a decision is made at the top and then passed down through the levels. I have found that my way of managing people works in a way that is inclusive and promotes a feeling of community within the team and the whole organization. This book is designed to help you to think in that way and become a leader that brings the whole team along.

I am going to share some experiences that may give practical tips that will help young executives to develop the analytical skills required for three-dimensional thinking at the strategic, tactical and operational levels. It is important to know how to develop your personal strategy in this area. The ideas and tips that I give you in this book will allow you to develop your skill set and make better decisions. The more you arm yourself with skill and knowledge then the better you will become. But before we hit light speed, let me first define strategic, tactical and operational to ensure we are speaking the same language.

Your business has important levels that define the impact of any decision or action that you take. In order to realize the consequence of any action you will need to understand these levels.

Strategic

The strategic level is usually associated with the whole picture of the company and how it defines its place in the world. It involves the directional decisions that a company makes and then the movement of resources to achieve these goals. For example the company's goals and the strategies put in place to achieve these goals would be seen as the company operating at the strategic level. Because of this the strategic level considerations are made for the medium and long term. You don't want an organization that changes it goals every six months! There are factors that can affect the strategic planning of a company and these tend to be mainly external. Changes in consumer behavior, changes in the market you are operating in or other external influences can have an effect on the strategic planning that a company implements.

Strategic planning and decision making affects everyone in the organization and because of this needs to be considered carefully. If the strategy shifts significantly then so does every other part of what the company does. The correlation between this and three-dimensional chess is strong because the decision will affect people at every level in every department. As with the example before when we looked at launching a new product, strategic changes bring about needs in the recruitment team, the training department, the marketing guys and the sales team as well as every other aspect of the company.

Senior management often makes these decisions, as it is their role to decide on the long-term future of the company. They have access to data from all the different parts of the organization and can collate this to see what is going on everywhere. These decisions are usually highly complex and will affect the entire direction that the company travels in.

Tactical

Tactical decisions are much more short term than strategic decisions. They are aimed at working out what each department must do to get to a specific goal in the future – usually about a year into the future at most. And in this is the other main feature that tactical decisions affect. They usually affect only a single department so each part of the company may well have a different tactical plan to get them to where they need to be. These tactical plans will all align with the overall strategic plan that defines where the company will be in 3 years time, 5 years time or even 20 years time but the tactical plan works pout how each part of the business will get to their shorter term goal.

Again there are potential uncertainties with tactical planning but they are much more short term than those faced in the strategic plan. They are more prone to be affected by staffing shortages for example where as in the long term these fluctuations are ironed out by the strategy that the organization passes down to the recruitment team. It can be said that the effective tactical plans are a series of steps that will get an individual department to where it needs to be in order to deliver their part in the overall long term strategic plan for the organization.

Middle management generally makes tactical decisions and they are less complex decisions but they still need to be considered and made carefully. They consider how to achieve the company goals in a more practical manner, but still have to have an eye on the strategic plan and the near future.

Operational

Operational planning and decision making is much more involved in the day to day of the business. They are related to the people, the processes and the systems that a company uses to deliver its products and service to customers. These are crucial decisions to the smooth operation of the company on that particular day and are totally department-specific but will only have one eye on the strategic plan that shows where the company needs to be in 20 years time.

The operational decisions made by a company are more often than not made by junior management and have an impact on the day to day running of the company. They are more often than not fluid and routine decisions that keep the operation moving along smoothly. Again, they sit within the framework of the strategic and tactical decisions but they are very much of their own particular point in time. They are made daily and can change daily too. For example, a decision to move one member of the sales team to help another today might not be replicated tomorrow or ever again.

Now you know the different levels of decision making that are found in an organization you will also probably be able to see where you fit into all of this. Your role at the moment will determine the impact of your decisions and the scope of the people you have to consider during all of this. Remember back to the three-dimensional chessboard. The decisions you make, whether strategic, tactical or operational will have an impact on two things. Firstly the future decisions that you can make from the position you now find yourself in. The second factor is the other 'players' in the game – your work colleagues.

OPERATIONS FOR THE MASSES

Now we have taken a look at the scale of the issue at hand here it is time to get down to some facts and see where you can take this. As you have seen in the first chapter, every decision has a knock-on effect for everyone else – certainly those in your immediate sphere of influence. Where you sit in the organization will have an influence on how you approach your decision-making and also how you deliver the effects of the decision making of others. The closer you are to the top of the food chain, the greater the opportunity that you may lose touch with the needs and wants of those at the bottom. If you sit at a place in the middle of the company (as I'm sure many of my readers actually do) then you have the twin effects of implementing the orders of others as well as making your own decisions that will affect your team either in the short term or on a day-to-day basis. It is you, the mid-level executive that makes the company you work for tick. You need to be the conduit that brings about great tactical solutions from the strategic messages that have been delivered to you in your position.

There is a line of command in many organizations that is quite linear in the way it operates. Great decisions are made at the head of the organization and then these are passed down the line to eventually reach those on the shop floor or customer facing roles. These are then the people that have to engage and interact with customers about these changes and

make them work. Think back to the example from the first chapter about a new product launch. If the product is launched as an edict from the managing director and then those in the company that deal with customers are just expected to deliver results then there is exposure to everything breaking down. The correct training may not be delivered, the customer agents may not have enough product knowledge to make the sales and they will feel unappreciated because they have been left adrift to find a solution to someone else's problem. Warp speed to request. Sometimes we miss the impact of our actions based on the demands of our leaders. We do what is asked of us without thinking about how it can be best achieved. Sometimes we think that those above us are paid to make these decisions and we are just here to pass them along the line. Think back to our chess game, as we move the bishop from the third tier board, what have we done to the pawn on the second or the knight on the first? This may not have been an important consideration for those at the top of the tree but your team are those that you have to motivate personally to achieve the results that your leaders expects from you. The pressure is on to make something happen even though you may not have the full understanding yourself to deliver the information in an effective and inspiring way to those on your team that need to move forward with the message. Communication is the key here but the whole system needs to have a specific strategic and tactical planning to deliver effective results for the company and its customers. You can easily get sucked into delivering what your leader requests without considering your next move and how it affects all the pieces on the three-dimensional chessboard that your organization resides in is. The effective leader of people can see all of the steps that are needed to deliver an effective solution to a new problem rather than just passing on what they have been told. And this is where a manager that knows their team and the personalities in it comes into their own. Each member of your team will react to change in a different way. From the methods that team needs the information to be delivered, in to how vocal they are about it. From the influence they have on others to their commitment to make it work. You as a middle manager will have developed a good idea of how your team will deal with all of this. In the modern business age change is inevitable. Strategic change may be as difficult to turn around as a battleship because it is about culture and beliefs, and you can't change people's beliefs in an instant. But tactical change may have to be delivered in a short period of time. In business, the year that tactical planning and decision making covers is really a very short space of time. Once you have delivered a message, deployed your training program, trained it out and embedded it as a standard normal practice, then half of that year is usually already up. But how effectively you put this change in motion (and how effective the change is to the business) depends to a large degree on personality and how these personalities are interconnected on the three-dimensional chessboard.

Back to how you deliver the change to your team. Every member of your team will look at things differently. Some want to ask every question under the sun as soon as they hear about the change being announced. Some need time to take it all in and would rather go away with it written down to mull it over and process it. Some need to have a good moan about it and get their frustration off their chest before settling down to a new routine. There are so many factors to consider and this is just to deliver that message. That is why you always need to consider that chessboard with every move you make. After delivering the message you also need to consult, ask for feedback, answer questions, make it happen, evaluate and feed back up the pyramid line. So you can see as every personality on your team meets with each of the three stepping-stones along the change path you will have to work out what you should do for the best. And that is where the good leader knows their team. They know which people need to approach the situation in which way; they know the people that need a few days to think about it. They know the people who will be able to influence others on the team. In other words they know the consequences of their next move, the one after that and the one after that as well. The good leader takes all of this into account when they convert strategic decisions into tactical and operational actions.

You see as you begin your journey (or your trek) keep in mind it is about today and immediate results. You will be measured on what you and your team can deliver to the company by the close of business tonight. But no move you ever make can be isolated from what you did yesterday or what you will do tomorrow. The quote is "tomorrow is another day" but it doesn't happen in isolation. The moves that you make in your three dimensional chess game still stand when you return to your desk tomorrow. The board isn't wiped clean. You do not start all over again. The whole of the organization you are working for is generally pulling in the same direction. The goal is the long term strategic place that the leaders heads of the company have decided you need to work to in 3 years time, 5 years time or even 20 years time. The role of a good leader is one that will get you to destination without leaving shrapnel as you move through your multiple verticals and horizontals. The pieces in this chess game can occupy the same square at the same time so when they are in close proximity a little friction can often occur. You as a leader need to make sure that this isn't carried over into the next work cycle. Again it is about knowing the personalities of the team and making sure that all the different elements of the team are well oiled and working well together.

There are many rules to follow in this game because it is as complex as the one Mr. Spock was playing all those years ago. You need to be a tactical genius to have played that game with Spock and an even greater one to have a chance of beating him. But as an executive in a company you have to think about the rules of the game that you have been presented with. Unless the game you are playing is about delivering to some monarchist king's wishes, then you will possibly feel that all rules are meant to be broken. But this is not the case. The rules are not in place to keep people in line. Great leaders develop a set of rules that allow everyone to flourish. Not the rules of a dictator that are designed to keep everyone down. That is no way to inspire people because it rules on the basis of fear rather than love and motivation.

You will probably hear some great war time quotes in the organization that you are working for from time to time. They are used in a way that is designed to inspire and get the team of workers behind a cause-

"It is better to ask forgiveness than permission"
"Speed is the key to success"
"The genius of the And"

Those quotes all have a place in a healthy working environment but it is in those toxic environments that you need to keep an eye on the Captain staff versus the staff Captain, as he/she may be the worm hole that will bring you to a dark and dreary environment. When you place all your eggs in the same basket you know what may happen. If you allow one person to make all the decisions without consultation or accountability then the same can happen to an organization. To have a company that looks to the needs of their team and the customers then some of the influence that guides the decision-making must come from that part of the company that has regular contact with customers. I once worked for a specialty retailer British Petroleum and one of the things that made them different in the way decisions were made was the fact that senior management of all levels had to spend a lengthy period of time 10 days every year working in one of their stores and in every department gas station forecourts dealing with the customers and working alongside the members of the team that had to deliver their tactical and strategic decisions. The result? Well the decisions that were made had much more consideration for the members of the team that they spent time with. If they implemented a new procedure they would easily find from feedback and practice if it didn't work. From there they could rescind or improve the procedural change to make it fluid and well received more workable for those team members and customers that it had affected.

Operations for the masses is all about the mission and most of the time not about the people. This is not the way to build a strong working relationship or to deliver the results that your end customer might need. It feels like everyone is pandering to the whim of an emperor and not having any practical input to make things better. The people are more important than the mission in many ways but the best way to reconcile the two is to ensure that they can both be delivered together. Again this is where a good leader of people is worth a huge amount to a progressive organization. A leader that knows the impact a change can have on their team and can then deliver this change in an engaging and positive way to the different people that work there is invaluable. That leader changes the situation from one of conflict to one of harmony. The best leaders always gravitate to good people and companies as they always find a way to connect and share their hearts with one another over time. They understand the three dimensional chess game that is at play and can take the necessary steps to bring everyone together to deliver the results that the company needs without foregoing the needs of the people that work there. This is where we are going with this book. This is how I wish to share MY heart with you. The message I want to convey.

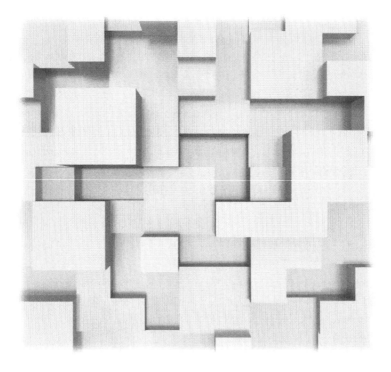

CAN OPERATIONS HAVE A NON-TRADITIONAL SHAPE?

The different parts of the organization that we have already looked at in this book may have to deal with change and decision making in different ways. Some departments are all about change such as research and development or marketing. Their every moment is dedicated to delivering change for other parts of the business and for customers. The parts of the business that face customers on a daily basis will see a degree of flux from different customers with different needs that require a different solution. Once these different solutions are delivered in an effective way then that customer leaves happy, the next one turns up and you figure out how to make this one happy. This is a continual line that gives the job role meaning and excitement every day.

Operations.... Well, we know what you have read, I am pretty sure what you have been told but here is a curve ball for you. Whatever you thought you knew things have changed. And even since they last changed, there are plans to change them again. You are at the part of your organization that powers through the strategic decisions and delivers them into tactical AND practical solutions that work for all the people around you. The operations managers at every level are most in the line when it comes to receiving the decisions of those above them and turning that into something practical and inspiring to get their team on board. The operations leaders need to know their team inside out and just make things happen in a way that is meaningful to the end customer. Don't work in operation if you are afraid of change and being the person to implement it. Change is at the heart of everything you do and it won't go away if you close your eyes for a few seconds, or even a few days.

It is nebulous, it is gray, and it takes shape based on your surroundings. When you think you have it figured out, the consumer, economy and even insecure leadership may take your perfectly designed (in your own mind anyway) process and give it a whirl. This is the very essence of operations because that is what you folks do. You take the situation as it is today and provide a solution that works. You take all the internal and external inputs and turn this feedback into a workable solution. You are the engine that drives the whole business forward, because if you ever stopped too long to think about the decisions you have to make then it would all probably grind to a halt. That doesn't mean that your decisions are unimportant, it just means that you have to make them while keeping everything else running. Unlike another department you can't stop all the wheels from turning while you settle on a solution and put it into place. You have team members waiting on your every word. You have customers at the end of the phone, in face-to-face situations, over the Internet and all the other platforms that you use to interact with your customer base.

Make peace with it either quickly or over a reasonable amount of time as you will need to acknowledge a word like, "change" or "amalgamation" or "different" or my favorite, "renaissance", or any other word that conveys the situation you are facing. The leader that does not embrace change will find that they get left behind really quickly. The leader that ignores change is doing a disservice to their team and to their customers. Change is an integral and an essential part of any organization. You see, an organization is a living thing that is full of moving parts and each part changes in some way at every interaction they have with another part of the organization or an external influence.

The economy in your home market, currency fluctuations, changing customer attitudes, the pressure from a competitor or any other one of a million differ variables can change the way that your company is perceived and indeed the way in which it operates. For example, if you suddenly have a competitor that is taking market share and loyal customers from you then the way in which your company operates will change to react to that situation. Where you once had little competition so you could focus on the benefits of your product or service with your customers you now have to take the rival into account. When talking to your customers you now have to show why you are better, point out the flaws in your competitor's product or service and have a completely different conversation with the same people. You have changed the way you do business. These types of changes occur in subtle (and less so subtle) ways in every market and every industry. The organization with the flexible operations team that can deliver the change in a way that engages and inspires their team AND their customers, win every time. The organization that sticks to their rigid patterns of the past will suffer and may eventually lose more and more market share. The company that refuses to change dies. The famous phrase, "we have always done it this way", is what will be etched on their mausoleum door.

A dynamic pile of clay that delivers results and can be what you want it to be is a lot more accepting and fun to work with than what you thought was a more militant way of managing. When it comes to working with your team you need to think of them in this way. They are not a series of bricks to be built up and to create a rigid structure. The way to inspire even soldiers is now changing as the army comes away from the old sergeant major screaming at the recruits scenario to something more inspiring and engaging. Leadership in all forms of life, is seeing a change in the way it is delivered and acted upon. Your teams of people are a diverse bunch of characters, as we looked at in the last chapter. They have earned and deserve a diverse bunch of solutions that give them a framework to deliver results but at the same time allow them to grow and think for themselves. As with the three-dimensional chessboard there are more moves than just forward and backwards. And each move that you make can be countered or followed by a seemingly infinite number of responses. The great leader will mold their team to respond to the challenges of that day, that week, that month or that year. Within the wider strategic plans that senior management have put in place there are more than one way of delivering a solution with a set number of people and a finite budget. You are the master of that team and you are charged with delivering a set result with the resources that senior management deemed appropriate. The next steps are all yours to take so choose them wisely and you can see positive outcomes. It is your remit as a leader of people to get the best out of that team. But you can't be alongside every member of your team every minute of the day to guide every single decision that they make. But that does not mean that you have no influence over what they do. The great leader will have a plan in place to ensure that their team knows exactly what is expected of them. The great leader leaves nothing in this area to chance but still gives the people in the team the opportunity to make their own decisions and deal with their own situations. It all starts with the culture that you develop and the way that you empower your people to make the decisions that you would have made but without your input at that particular moment in time. Speak to your team on a regular basis, share your heart with them, especially at times of real change (and we know as operations managers that this is almost always!) so you can lead them to the place you want them to be. The great leader is always able to communicate the values that they have and how they want these values to be represented. They say that a team operates in the image of its leader and this is totally true. Enable your team to operate in the image you have created and you will see that they pull together to deliver the tactical planning decisions you have made and implement them operationally as you desire. This is not another form of dictatorship but a program of training, mentoring and coaching that gets your team to the place you want them to be. They still have the autonomy to make individual decisions but they also know the guidelines and expectations that the company, you as their line manager, their colleagues and their customers expect from them. Who said the square peg always has to fit in a square hole? No peg, no hole just space and creativity to get things done all within a timeline, budget and people at the forefront of your formula. This is the way that you should see your management role in the organization you are operating in. Like your team you know as an executive what the company expects, what its values are and how they want to be seen. After that the decisions are yours to make, yours to take the credit for and you to sort out if they go wrong. But don't let this sound like an invitation to pass on responsibility for making decisions or to avoid making them at all. You need to be the heart of your team and be seen to lead your people into battle. On the chessboard you don't see a set of 16 pawns and no king. You see a team of people with different skills and different abilities that work together to achieve an objective. Take this step further to the three dimensional chessboard and you will see how this can apply to a company or department of any size or shape. Sandboxes are meant to be played in and not be used as jail cells. The quicker you grasp that piece, the less angst you will go through in your professional career. The areas that your organization must spend the most money on are those that empower your team to collaborate, develop new systems and take the company forward. These need to be places to play, explore and develop as an individual and as a team. The last things these places need to be are restrictive or confining. The organization that succeeds in the future will get there because they have allowed their team the freedom to develop innovative solutions that match both internal and external customer needs. This is much more preferable to the organization that wants every task delivered in a strict and defined manner that has been passed down from senior leaders who are by definition at least a little out of touch with customers. Operations isn't just something that can have a non-traditional shape, it is something that by definition needs to be able to reshape into non-traditional ideas every working day and week of the year. Your customers will change regularly, the external factors that influence your industry change all the time so the solutions you provide MUST also be able to take non-traditional forms when the conditions require. Operations managers have figured all of this out some time ago but the message needs to go back up the pyramid. The market is changing. Customer behaviors are changing. Your competitors are changing. This is more than ever a case of whoever is standing still is actually falling behind. I implore you to think about all of this in the proper context. I have been effective because I can see how the three-dimensional chess game affects all of those around me. We can see from operations that this game also includes your customers, external factors and your competitors. The game just got even more complicated. But don't sweat it. You are doing something about it. By reading this book you will hopefully walk away with ideas that can help you and your team to move forward as a group. The executive that becomes armed with information is the one that will lead the way in the future.

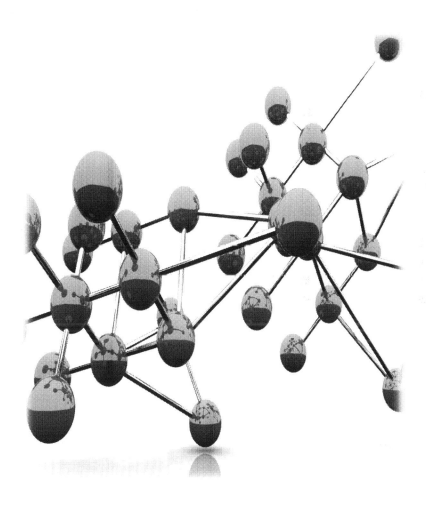

CONNECTING THE DOTS AND MOVING INTO TACTICAL SPEAK

The space that you occupy in your organization is unique. You have your own place on the three-dimensional chessboard and the moves that you make ripple through the other players. You must not let the fact that you know your moves have a consequence to paralyze you into inaction. The player that is aware of the rest of the game can sometimes not want to make the next move in case he or she sets off a chain of actions that they cannot control any longer. But remember that others on the chess board will be making moves all the time – whether they are aware of the other players or not. This makes the game something continual and something that happens all the time whether you have an input or not. You can't press pause. You can't bail out. You can't ask for a time out. The game goes on whether you make your move or not. Nobody waits for you to make up your mind if it is going to hold them back from what they need to do. The modern organization is a series of interconnected departments that all need to come together to reach their goals. The modern organization is full of small niches and areas of expertise that merge to achieve the overall goals of the company. And different characters manage all of this individually. Everything they do needs to have the end customer in mind always.

Well now we are really moving through space. We are able to touch what someone is dreaming about and begin to look past what is in front of you and actually see what you may be lead to believe is strategy? Ah nope, not yet. You are now getting the opportunity to move out of a task or multi task environment and hear how the vision "sort of" touches what you do and how you do it. But that does not mean that you are failing. Your place in the organization and the influence that this brings are always present. You have the power to make a positive impact on those around you by considering your moves and making them wisely. There will be large areas in your organization that are filled with nothing. There are places that you can move to that will allow you to build your own style, gather your own people and move forward to driving that team to success. The guys at the top will develop their strategic plans and then often just walk away and expect them to be delivered. They pass on the general ideas to the next level of management and then wait for the results to be reported back. They don't divorce themselves from all responsibility in this area but they do delegate large amounts of it. They look to the middle management teams to drive these strategic goals into tactical plans because these are the people that they have recruited and promoted to drive this forward. As a middle executive you have proven yourself worthy to deliver these results from your past actions or the strength of your resume. Now is the time to deliver.

The organization you are working in is a complex thing. It has many moving parts that don't always interconnect in the most efficient way. Teams are lead by personalities and these personalities can get in the way of true efficiency. Don't try to take the personality out of it all because this is not what we are all about. You need to develop working relationships with these characters because they occupy a space on the chessboard. If all trains were efficient and worked in exactly the way that the strategists at the top wanted them to then there would be no place for people like you. Organizations never work in this way, which is why you can find your own niche, and develop a set of skills and relationships that make you stand you from the crowd. You are different because you work in a different way. You are successful because you have come to learn the impact of your decisions and the way that you need to play the game. Considering the consequences of your actions means that you take the personality of others into account. Think back to when you had to implement a new product or initiative. The personality of others determined how you presented the change, how you trained in the change and how you delivered the change. The same goes when dealing with other chess pieces with a similar standing to you. Just because you are now a knight and come across another knight it doesn't mean you play the game in a different way. You still look 5 moves ahead, 10 moves ahead, 20 moves ahead or more and play the game in the exact same way. The potential consequences may be more complex but the game remains the same.

You see, embracing the grey space is allowing you to understand how to pull things together and solve for larger problems that are lost behind a lot of noise and commonly called blank space dilemmas. It is all about filling the gap between what has been expected of you and the results that you deliver. A blank space dilemma is the place in space and time that you fill with your skills and expertise. This is where you start playing the game of three-dimensional chess in earnest. You need to consider the results that you are required to deliver, the timeframe that you have to do this in and the resources you have at your disposal. The expert chess player sees many moves ahead to make the right decisions now. You have to see all the moves ahead (as far as you possibly can) until that deadline approaches. What might delay you? Who in your team will be best positioned to get you over the line? Do you need extra resources? Are these extra resources available? These are some of the thousands of question that bounce around in your head at the outset. The great chess player needs a tactical plan. And they need a tactical plan that can be implemented at the grass roots level. As you can now see more clearly than ever, you are the link between understanding the strategy, making a tactical plan and then implementing it operationally. You are the conduit that changes ideas into actions and actions into results. This is now your place in the company and this is the way you can take things forward.

Every move you make has an impact on others. We have seen this from start to finish in this book and we see it every day in our working lives and beyond. The truly great chess player can assess the situation quickly and come up with a plan straight away to deliver the results that they want. If you or I sat across from a grand master then we would lose ten times out of ten. And our opponent would have planned most of our losses out after our first few moves. But you are far more experienced in your business life than behind a chessboard. You have had experiences of just about every situation. Don't forget, that experience can come in many different forms. You can have the practical experience of having been through something similar on many occasions before. You can have the theoretical experience of having known a situation, spoken to others about it or read it in a textbook or online. This doesn't give you the same hands-on experience but it allows you to understand in concept and principle what is going on and make a better decision. You can pool the experience and knowledge of your team because they may have seen this situation before many times. You don't just have to rely on what you have done before. Innovative solutions that pool the resources of those around you and deliver results will make you and your colleagues stronger and boost confidence that you know you can work together to solve whatever comes your way. The team that fills those voids of grey space will be the team that drives your organization to a successful and prosperous future. Be the leader of that team.

Whether anyone from senior management acknowledges it or not, the strategic plans they send out are flawed. They must be flawed by very definition. They cover the long-term future of the company and provide the broad-brush strokes of what they have considered and want to be delivered. The plans have to leave out vital information and instruction because a plan that covers every detail that the company needs to know for the next 20 years will just be out of date before it hits the desks of the relevant people. But that is how it works. The strategy broadly points the ship in the right direction. The tactical planners make sure each part of the ship is geared up to get it all moving. And the operational people make it happen. But this is where the opportunity lies for success. You are the person who can gather all the right information from your network and create a working tactical plan that is not short on information or instruction. That is your role in the company. You take the unfilled plans of those at the top and deliver them into something workable that the operations team can make great use of. This is where the skilled three dimensional chess player really comes into their own. You take a lack of clarity and make it clear. You take a lack of information and make it informative. And all the while you are keeping the needs and wants of your team, the rest of the organization and the customers at the front of your thinking. You are now truly working on a different level. You are the spark of energy, enthusiasm and ability that drives things forwards. And as you see this you are also driving forward one other thing – your career.

Think of what your day was like when you walked in before the sun came up and knew the work load you had to muscle through. Now really roll up our sleeves because you are going to begin to see how to touch multiple layers in your space and move into the second chessboard. Keep your eye on the bishop below you as you may take out a great operational contributor by getting ahead of yourself. You need to keep making plans after every move. Don't let planning slow you down or make your team inefficient. You need to be quick to act but also act in a way that has been considered for what impact it will make. The leader that sees the opportunity to grow and does so in an effective way will soon move up the corporate ladder and take like-minded people with them. You need to connect the dots from strategy to operation and do so in a tactical manner. You are the person that makes all of this happen because that is what you are great at. Get those instructions and turn them into actions. I will help you to get there.

You can now start to see as we go through this book that your job is about more than your job. What you do resonates around the whole organization, not just the four walls of your office. You make a massive difference in the lives of others because you are changing their day. The decisions you make today will make the difference between success and failure. What you deliver at the end of the year has to be reported back to your line manager in your annual review. What you deliver at the start of the year determines how easy it is for your team to get you to the right place. The game is being played all the time. What you do every day in your job is tactical..."plan for it."

WE ARE MOVING ON UP

As you develop the skills and the foresight to lead a team and consider the implications of your moves on the rest of the organization you will become noticed and appreciated. Your line manager will understand the impact you are having on the team and see that you are rewarded. Firstly, this reward will be praise then it will be financial in the form of bonus payments and pay rises. Eventually the executive that plays the game of three-dimensional chess in the right way gets to move up the organization in terms of promotion. You start to feel that all you have learned in this book is paying off and you are achieving what you set out to. I am very happy for you. I genuinely want this for each and every one of my readers. The journey is not a short one, but what journey of any significance is? Anything that is worth having is worth fighting for. Anything that you really want is worth learning for, developing skills for and becoming the best at.

This is all part of your personal and professional development and you need to take responsibility for it. Investment in your career and investment in you as a person can go hand in hand. You don't leave behind the skills you learn at work when you clock out and get in the car for that commute home. You don't leave skills behind if you up and move to another company. These are all investments in YOU. The way that you play the game of chess has a huge standing on how you progress and how quickly you progress. Become the chess player that understands the game and play it in a manner that gets you moving through the company in a timeframe that suits your ambitions. I know that you are ambitious because you have taken the time from your busy life to read this book. You want to get better and you want to know how to get to the next level of the chessboard. Together we are going to make sure that you understand what to do and how to get there.

You are now moving toward the top of the mountain (so to speak), slowly but surely you will be invited into closed-door meetings, team assessments. YOUR OPINION will now begin to carry some weight. You feel as though the hard work you have put in is starting to pay off. You have worked to get to this level so enjoy it. But don't let that enjoyment cause you to sit back. This is a continual journey and the game of three-dimensional chess is not over just because you have moved up a level on the board. You are still involved in the game and the effects of your moves are now under much more scrutiny than they were before. The tactics that you employed to get to this level still apply for the moves that you make in the future. You still have to consider the impact of your actions on all others. Your move still needs to keep an eye on those that work in customer-facing roles and the customers they serve. But you are perfectly equipped to make these decisions and get them right every time. You have had the benefit of having those exact same considerations in the role you were in before and you still have the contacts to sound this out again. This is what sets you apart from the rest. This is your competitive advantage when it comes to being promoted and reaching the top of the mountain. You can't afford to become complacent when you are playing the game that never sleeps. Even if you take a few days, a few weeks, a few months to wallow in the glory of a promotion then you will find that when you return to the board all the pieces have moved and you are not really familiar with the location of all the important pieces. Don't take your eye off the game because it won't wait around for you to catch up again. You have to pick up where you left off.

Now comes the project ownership part of the tactical layer of your growth. Do not take it for granted, these are golden nuggets. Ensure to commit and go, "all in" on everything that you do, PEOPLE are counting on your success and most importantly...YOU. As you move onwards and upwards through the organization you will take others with you. As you find people that will give you support in all the right areas as well as challenge you when you need it then you want these colleagues to come along on the journey with you. They will become your trusted lieutenants that you will be able to lean on in certain situations. The people that work around you will also lean on you when they need help with an issue or want someone to discuss a problem with. You have made yourself an indispensable part of the organization and your network of contacts know that you can be relied upon because of your experience, your expertise and they learn over time that you can play the game of three dimensional chess. The way that you treat others and consider the impact of your decisions on them allows you to stand out from the crowd of others in the company. You got here because of doing what is right when no one is watching with a high level of integrity, remember that. Whether they explicitly know you are able to play this complex chess game or they just have a feeling about the way you operate will depend on their own level of self-awareness and personal development. But you know that all you do will keep you at the forefront of peoples' minds when they look for someone to help them. Always be that person wherever you are in the organization. Don' let those connections and your empathy fade away just because you have moved up a level or two. You always need to remember the others in the company and how they have to deliver their own part in the company's success.

Do not take a myopic view of the projects you are presented with, look beyond them and all of the pieces they touch. It can be easy to step away from the day-to-day operations part of the company and forget about the operation. Everything that goes through your hands ends up on the shop floor, on the coalface and in the laps of your customers. If they don't like what you do, or the operational team can't deliver it effectively then it will be a failure. And all eyes will be on you to explain why that actually happened. In all walks of life prevention is better than the cure. The projects you deliver are just the same. To clear up the mess and point the finger of blame (also known as the traditional corporate coat of arms) after something has failed takes time, energy and negativity that is difficult to muster. To plan properly, involve all affected parties and consider the effects of your decisions is a much more positive, inclusive and efficient way to operate. Remember you have spent many years in the operational level to be able to touch and see most things; this is where that hands-on experience gives you the upper hand. You can shine in this area by making the most of the fact you have done the role. You can empathize with the people in operations that have to get results from tactical plans. You can make your plans the best they have ever seen and make their job as easy to deliver as you can. From there you all share in the glory that surrounds that success. You are the one person that they can look and think, "I know they will look after me because they know what it is like. They know how tough it can be. They know what I need. They always put people first and mission always."

The mission is always important because the organization you work for will have shareholders and owners that always keep their eyes firmly on the results that are delivered. You can't operate in an environment where the results are unimportant as long as the people are happy. But remember that these are not exclusive things. You don't need to make people unhappy to get the right figures for the shareholders. The best results are always delivered by a team that understands what is expected, that are challenged to deliver a testing goal and are motivated and rewarded to do it. The mission has to be what happens at the end (and is planned for at the start) but the key piece bit in the middle is all people. You must have a motivated bunch of individuals that are well informed and able to pull together when you need or want to get results. You are the perfect person to make that happen because you have been delivering this for so long now. You know the personalities involved and how your chess moves will impact on them. You know from experience that if you move your piece in one way that your colleague will move theirs in another. Synergy of moves can help you to achieve your goals in a much more efficient and long-lasting way. When you find other three-dimensional chess players in your organization then stay in touch with them as regularly as you can. These are going to be the people that help you take your game to the next level. These are the people that will work with you to deliver the plans and changes that are needed on this journey. You will be sat alongside them at the higher levels of the company one day because, like you, they know how their decisions affect others and make the right decisions for all.

Stay humble, centered and focused. That is my endearing piece of advice to you from this chapter. You have got this far by playing the game in a manner that considers others. Just because you have reached a certain point then this is really not the time at all to stop playing the game. They say in business and politics that you need to be nice to people on the way up because you will need them again on the way back down. And this is often true. If you stop playing there dimensional chess in a considerate way just because you feel you have 'made it' then you won't stay nor deserve to be at that level for long. And certainly you won't be moving up to the next level after that. The reason that you are making your way in the company is because you became adept at considering others with your decisions. Don't stop making all the right decisions now. It is time to take things to the next level and get to the room where all decisions are made in the organization.

The next step for you in your journey is one towards the higher echelons. You go from making operational decisions in the past to tactical ones now. The only place to go is up as you look to become a senior part of the team. The way that you have got here still applies. You will always need to consider every move in terms of the impact on others. You will always need to have your eyes on that chessboard. The next step can be a massive one for someone who is unprepared. But preparedness is something that you have been doing all along. You are at a different level of the three-dimensional chessboard but all of your moves still have consequences. It may be a long way down to the lower levels of the board but you must adjust your vision so you can still see all the way to the bottom. Things will still happen there, so extend your network, work on a plan to see the whole board and let's go on with our journey. You stride forward onto strategy.... your final destination is to get to the TOP of our chessboard

ON TOP OF THE CLOUDS MOM

The journey continues. You move up through the levels from making operations actions, to tactical planning and now you are in a place where you can dictate the strategy of the organization. But I use the word "dictate" in a very loose form. You need to remember everything that got you here in terms of the impact you have on others. Being able to dictate direction does not in any way mean you change your style from enabler to dictator. With every move you make you are now working from a level where you and your actions will impact people at every level of the organization in every way. From the height you are now operating from, it is a long way down to the customer and those that directly serve them but in no way can your actions, efforts and decisions be detached from those that matter.

Everything you do must be considered in exactly the same way. You are still playing three-dimensional chess but some of the pieces are so far away they are almost out of view. You and the people around you need to make sure that all the pieces are still in play and you never lose sight of where they are. This is the way that an effective senior manager goes about their business. You must find a way to keep in touch with the people that matter – your customers. Remember the company I mentioned in an earlier chapter where the top executives worked in every department every year? It made sure that they stayed in touch, stayed relevant and made decision that they knew would work.

You have arrived. Things here will look different, feel different and also sound different. Now you will need to remember the most important gift that was granted to you, which lead you down this path (or up these stairs). "CHARACTER". Character is doing the right thing when no one is looking..."remember that? Character is what you have developed over your time in business. It consists of all the things that you want others to see (and all of the things that perhaps you don't) because it is what has got you here. It looks and feels quite different to the character you had when you first started out in business because you have developed and learned along the way. The quality executive that turns into the great leader will develop their skill set to become better and better each day, week, month and year. By reading this book you are setting out on a path of self-improvement. Your character is the one thing that you can rely on when times are tough. It is the very essence of you and is so important that you should bottle it and sell it. The character of the leader is a valuable commodity. Don't dilute yours for the needs or demands of others. You are a strong character who has made it this far because of the strength of your beliefs and the caring nature that you bring to the workplace. This does not stop as you move up the levels; in fact it needs to get stronger. You may work alongside people that don't see the game in the same way that you do. They might try to tell you that you have to operate differently now, that you don't need to think about those below, that you have made it. But this isn't the way to get ahead and certainly isn't the way to provide the right solutions for the whole organization and the customers. Don't forget who you were and are and don't worry so much about being part of the, "club", they eventually all fade away anyway. Focus on people and achievement. This is what helps to keep you grounded and connected to all the right people. It is less important to be part of a clique or popular by ceding way with others. It is far more important to be respected for doing the right things and being that person that people go to when they need guidance, structure and development. As the others that thought they were making progress by being popular fade away you will remain standing as the person who kept things in perspective and delivered when it was needed. You did this by being aware of the chessboard at all points. Considering the consequences of your actions made your moves and as such you built up a network in the company of people that know you as the "go to guy and one of the good guys." You have built up an internal and external team around you of people that you know you can trust to deliver the results you require. Rely on this team and trust them to deliver as they have done in the past. Reward them for their loyalty and see that they generate a similar team around them as they move up through the levels of the company. Their network becomes your network.

Start looking around and down the chessboard. It will have 3 times the pieces, complexity and the audience will be unsure of you as a player for a while. Remember, just when you think that you have thought big enough, think bigger. The game gets bigger and bigger the further up the levels you travel. You become more aware of the other departments, divisions and competitors that might not have been in your eye when you were purely based in operations. You have a greater sphere of influence both internally and externally because as you rise higher in your organization you have more people report into you and collaborating with you. You have more pieces every day as your success drives the company forward. The better you get at the game of three-dimensional chess then the harder it becomes. But at the same time, the harder it becomes the better you are at playing the game. Your rise through the company or the industry was no fluke. It is based in your ability to play this game perfectly. Bear that in mind as you move up the levels. Here is where you still sponge as a student and process as a mad scientist. Don't speak PhD, as folks may think you are either arrogant or intimidating based on their insecurity or uncertainty. You need to communicate effectively. Everything you learn at one level needs to be effectively communicated at every other level in the organization and with your customers. For example, if you learn about a new supply chain process from your six sigma team that will lead to a new speed to market initiative then the way you consume and deliver this information is critical to the success both internally and externally – with customers. Your team that works in the sales channel wants to know what it does differently and how they can sell it, marketing wants to know what messages to deliver to customers, the training department wants to know how they can effectively deliver the program they need to quickly execute the process. None wants to know the science behind it. Make sure that you can take information from one source and think about how another audience will react to it. We are back to consequences and impact. Remember you are still playing chess.

As you devise, contemplate and deliver plans for the rest of the organization you will have to work harder in some areas to see if they will be effective. As I have mentioned, you are now further from the lower levels of the organization and in many way further from the end customer. You need to make plans to get to see these levels whenever you can. Sitting in an office looking at nothing other than four walls does not keep you connected. Sure, you have a strong network that you have built up during your time with the company but nothing beats seeing what is going on with your own eyes. Keep open the lines of communication with all those that you have worked with in the past. A promotion to the higher echelons of the company does not make you a different person (and it certainly does not make you a better person) but it makes you a person that has greater influence. Use that influence for the best to deliver positive outcomes for all those involved. Speak to your operational teams to see what it is that is stopping them from delivering. I once worked with a business owner who operated by seeking out information from his teams. Every department he walked into he asked "is everything OK?" and the reply every day was "no problems, boss." But when he went out to see customers they were reporting problems left, right and center. He hadn't inspired his teams to give him the information he needed. He had become this boss who was so powerful that it was a thing of shame to tell him you had a problem. His teams wanted him to know everything was fine because they feared telling him they had an issue or needed help. Don't become that type of boss. Listen to what people are telling you. Encourage them to let you know what is going on and then provide solutions. The way that you solve their problems will determine how many problems they are willing to bring you in the future.

You also need to give consideration to the fact that sometimes, although you do all things as best you can, you will have insecure or threatened leaders that may or will come after you. These leaders will see your success and become jealous of what you do and the way you do it. Instead of learning from you or partnering with you some will try to shut you down, discredit you or even try to force you out. You may end up having to leave or be asked to leave as the culture has given you a road that ends because they don't see your style as a fit. There are walls that certain people have built up in organizations when they have been there for a long time. They create their own little kingdoms and see threat to these everywhere. The way they have always worked is successful for them and this is all they ever wanted. It can be a painful time and you may think that there is no way back but the success story here is you. The skills and behaviors that you have developed and displayed will keep you in good standing wherever it is that you work. You need to ensure that you operate in an inclusive, caring and positive way to get to your goals, never be dragged down into the sordid way that these megalomaniacs go about their business. Generate relationships with others by the way that you operate and for the benefit of both parties. Never cultivate relationships on the basis of what you can get out of someone or to further your own career to the detriment of theirs. The way that you treat others will come back to you in the way that they treat you. When you need a favor then you want to be able to ask someone who you have helped in the past – not someone that you have bled dry.

Balance your time, energy and emotions. They are precious resources and you only have so much to go around. Focus professional time on YOU, team, leadership and company. Exactly in that order OR you will be no good to anyone if you are last in this equation. You have to be the leader of the team and to do that you have to develop professionally and learn every day. The rest will follow as you get better and better at what you do. If you have a team that knows what is expected of them then this has come from you knowing first what you expect of yourself. When you put yourself first in terms of professional development then you are in the ideal position to help and guide others. If you put yourself last in this equation then you will never become a better leader and things will start to fall apart. These people are looking to you for leadership and guidance so you really had better make sure you are in a position to give them that.

We have travelled a long way together but don't think that the journey is about to end. Now let's get to the good stuff...

THERE IS NO TIMER FOR THE NEXT MOVE

You have moved your way up the different levels and reached the level you set out for at the start of your journey. The start of this path was full of everyday considerations of the operational side of things as you worked the day-to-day side of the company. This was a great grounding in what it means to deliver results when you are face to face with customers. From there you continued your journey to making tactical decisions at the middle management level. You were able to easily consider the impact that these decisions had on operations because it was where you started. You still had a great network of contacts there and were able to consider the consequences of your actions. You became the conduit that took broad strategic plans from the senior management team and made these into workable solutions for the operations teams. This was your forte because you had the right way of making the pieces move on that three dimensional chessboard. You were able to consider what the impact of your next move was and plan many moves ahead. You could see all the pieces in site and predict accurately what they would do in reaction to your move. Then as you used your skills and knowledge to continue the game you were able to move onwards and upwards within your organization or industry. You have reached the level of senior management. The game in parts is a little more difficult to play because some of the operational pieces are a long way below you and difficult to spot. But your network and the people you spend time with allow you to keep in touch and make the decisions that have a positive impact on all parts of the business. That is how you got here and that is how you will remain successful.

Welcome to where people's career are now truly in your realm of influence and responsibility. You are the master of your own domain and people rely on you. The more successful you are, the more secure their job is. The more you rise up to the c-levels of the company, the more chances they have of being promoted. The better you deliver the results that are required of you, the better pay and bonus they can expect. There is a lot riding on your success. But, as before, don't let this weigh you down. You have gotten to this level because of your own character, your own determination and your own ability to improve. Continuous improvement is what marks out the great leaders from all the others. The great leader sees every day as an opportunity to learn and get better. The great leader sees opportunity in every situation. The opportunity to get better at what you do appears in front of you every day, but many are too centered on their own life to see it. The great leader always has their eyes open to see what might happen. They always have the benefit of their team and the organization in their eye line. As you move your way through the company you will see that people look up to you. Not in terms of blind admiration or a sense of authority, but because you have been a part of their success. They realize that without you they may not have had the same opportunities to grow. They realize that without you they may not be where they are in their career. They realize that without you their prospects may be slightly different. But that past history of success leads to a future expectation of more success. The great leader stands on their last result. The game of three-dimensional chess is still being played and more pairs of eyes with every successful move you make are watching the way that you play it. It is like the successful craps player at the casino (but nothing about your career is chance) because every time you roll the dice and win, the number of people that are drawn to the table to watch grows. As you continue on a winning streak (not a lucky steak) then more people are drawn to you and are aware of you. They want to see how you get on, and how it will affect them. Every chess move becomes more difficult and its repercussions more impactful. As your power and sphere of influence grows then the number of people that can and will be impacted by what you do grows too. It makes sense. When you were working operationally you may have been responsible for around 30 people. As you move up the chessboard and reach senior management then the number of people reporting in to you might have grown beyond the hundreds and into the thousands. That is a lot of careers and livelihoods that you are now accountable for. That is a lot of people that might struggle financially and psychologically if the company suffers a shock and has to make people redundant, for example. You need to keep up your side of the bargain with the people above you and the people below you. The people above you saw potential in you. They noticed the results that you were delivering and, if they were any good at their job, also noticed the way that you created these results. Just putting numbers on a piece of paper is one thing, but achieving these figures hy going about things in an efficient and effective manner is something else completely. Then the people below you have brought into what you bring to the table and your idea of where the company, the department or the operation should go. We are back to the three levels of decision-making in terms of strategic, tactical and operational. The people that have worked with you and followed you on this journey have made a bargain with you in a way that they expect you to keep on delivering. Not only delivering the success that secures their jobs and earns them a good bonus. This is also the success that has come about of working in the right way. The success that has seen your team follow you up the different levels of the three dimensional chess board as they believe in your principles and follow your lead. You are the leader of this group and it is up to you to remain strong.

You will need to focus on two questions that will be at the forefront of **all of who you are** from here on in-

"How do I evaluate and develop my team to support the potential redesign of the organization?"

 Yes, from your level of influence and oh yes, contraction and expansion can happen quickly around you. This is a question of embracing all that happens to make a better world for you, your team, your company and your customers. We knew all about external factors when we worked in operations. We knew that things changed on a regular basis and we dealt with it. The messages that came down the line needed to be implemented to get the 20-year strategic plan into a one-year tactical plan and to a daily operation. And we just made it happen because that is what operations do. But back in those days we wanted to know what those up the pyramid were doing for us. We wanted to know that they had considered us in their decision-making. Well, guess what? That same attitude that you had still exists in the operations teams today. The people there will make things happen but just like you did, want to know how you could help them. Like the quality leader you are, this means that you want to make it as easy as possible for everyone in the organization to deliver what is expected of them.

This means that you are still keeping the game of chess going for everyone. You may make the plans that work their way down the chain but you know that chain like the back of your hand because it wasn't that long ago that you worked there yourself. This means that you understand the different components that go into making it successful. Let's take that example of a new product launch again. You know that it won't be successful if you just launch it and expect the whole company to catch up in their own time. This wouldn't be strategic thinking – it would be setting the whole organization up for failure. You know that to be successful you need to persuade all parts of the company that this is a great product that will increase sales. You need to do an internal marketing campaign before you even let the first customer see it. There then will be training issues to make sure that all the teams know what it does and how to sell it. Marketing need to do their job, there may be recruitment needs; the list goes on and on. That is when you need to evaluate the starting point and then develop that into a series of solutions to make this new product a success. You won't do this alone but you have already become the expert in this by the way you play their dimensional chess. This is just an extension of that game that gives you the challenge you need to keep your skills at the highest level.

"Where is or are the industries I touch headed?"

This is more about you than it is about your company. It is your personal responsibility to keep on top of this every day. It is known as continuous professional development and is a highly important part of all that you do. With your development you look at what your industry is doing as well as what you and your team are doing. If you were a retailer 15 years ago and went on a program of development that made you the best retailer physical brick and mortar retailer you could be, then you would have been left behind. While you were busy becoming the best physical brick and mortar retailer, online retail has thrived (and is now outselling brick and mortar or 4-wall physical retail stores shops) and you would have lost out. The industry changed in many ways over the last 15 years and if you did not keep your eye on where it was going, then you will miss vital information that can help your team, your company but most importantly you. There may be times when all the signs are bad. Your sources and the information you gather may indicate that your industry or your own company are heading for a major shock. The informed leader knows that they have a decision to make. They either have to start to look elsewhere or steer the company towards a safer place. But that only comes by knowing what is going on.

These two questions will have multiple versions over the next 20-30 years of your career. They are something that you need to consider often and keep an eye on constantly. Change will happen in every industry and company on an almost constant basis. There is no standing still in business. To take the retail example above, you will have been made irrelevant by an Amazon large E-retailer and your business won't exist anymore. You need to keep on top of these two things for the sake of your team and you. You need to know that you can move with the times and have a group of employees that are adaptable to what the customer requires. Customers will change their demands with trends, with a change in the economic environment and with changes in technology. The leader that understands this and gets together a team of people that can deliver when the time is right for change is the leader that gets the best results time after time. Change and the positive attitude towards it are cultural. It is bred in everything that a company does. It is in the workforce and in the customer base. You need to embrace change and develop a culture where your entire team embraces change as well.

So what should be the next move? Where should you go from here? What can you do to keep improving day after day, year after year? Here is where ministry comes in, strengthening those that want to be stronger and guiding those that don't know they need the help. You are the shining light when it comes to this. You have been that shining light for such a long time that people in your organization know where you are. Like a lighthouse they can look to you to steer away from rocky times. This is the role that you have created for yourself in the company and it is a hugely vital role when it comes to developing the way you all operate around each other. You are an enabler that allows others to get the best from themselves. You need to look around and seek out the colleagues that can benefit from your wisdom. Those are the chess pieces that require more attention and time until they are big enough and strong enough to not need your direct involvement. This does take time. It is not always easy to empower others to take responsibility for their own actions. Many want to learn and become better at what they do. This is the same attitude and way of working that got you to where you are now. But you will find others that would much prefer to leave responsibility in the hands of others and not become engaged. Never give up but open your heart to them. Let them know the power of sharing. You can make a huge difference to them not only at work but also in their life as a whole.

The next move is to look at all your decisions in terms of the bigger picture. It was easy to think day to day when you were in an operational role but those days are gone. You have to judge how wise your decision is now based on what it might do to sales, to customers and to the organization in 3 years time, 5 years time, 10 years time or even 20 years time. You have to consider whether your decision will mean greater job security for your team or the potential of redundancy. These are all "big picture" decisions that will shape the way you make them. As long as you have the whole picture and not just the bottom line in mind then you can make those choices for all the right reasons and be much more confident of success. The way that you connect, communicate and engage others is vitally important to the success of your message. You will already carry with you a certain authority because you have traveled a path and you have a senior position. But that is not everything. There is more to come from you. You need to use the advantages you have built to the greatest effect. You need to use the voice you have to positively influence others to think in the same way. You need to connect with people in a way that means something to them. Now the commoner's way of evaluation, no books, PhD's just good old fashion, "listening with your heart and hearing with your ears."

A LEADER'S ASSESSMENT

As your journey continues then you become more renowned in your job role. You may well go from being another member of the team to being a figurehead or personality either within your own organization or within the industry you work. This can bring benefits in terms of the standing and influence you have with your peers or across the whole industry. That three-dimensional chess board just got a whole lot bigger! Consider the reactions to what you say and do now in terms of the impact it could have on other companies as well. You have other chessboards to look at while you are making moves on yours. The game got really interesting for you. Just don't forget that it never stops whether you find time to keep an eye on it or not. And this is where the challenge can really lie when you reach this position of power and influence. As you look to lead your organization and perhaps your entire industry to new heights then you must make sure that you have the time to still see what is happening on the lower levels of the chessboard. Don't lose sight of the game because the people around you depend on you being able to play it effectively. When you reach this level you will almost always be known as a leader, but what is the point of that title if you are not going to lead? Leading means taking others with you. It does not mean that you do only what is in the interest of those around you at board level. You have much more people to consider than that. The three dimensional chessboard is deep and you have made sure that you have the right contacts to touch all parts of it. Remember, "Leadership is a privilege and NOT an entitlement."

You will now need to really pay attention to the message within the conversation. People will say things they want you to "feel their emotional highs and lows" without sharing their hearts with you. You are the center of attention for many people in your company and they will all rely on you in some degree or another to lead them to success. You will need to begin to do the work that you were blessed to do…. LEAD as an empathetic leader. You must continue to have the style that has got you here- fair, firm and with a high level of integrity. Yes, it will not give you many fans in the board room but you have already acknowledged you have a higher calling so by now you will have made peace with it. The work that you do and the decisions that you make are all part of the same plan you had when you started out. Your integrity has seen to it that you will always keep the customer and the employees at the heart of all your decisions and actions. Empathy is something that many who make it through the system and rise to the top of the pyramid ignore because they don't feel it is necessary for their own self-interest any more. But you are different. You know what it is like to work up through the different levels of the organization and you know what works for other people. You are the shining light that delivers great results by working out what is right for everyone involved, not just those the shareholders or company owners. Everyone who works there has an emotional and practical stake in the organization and all want it to succeed. Those that have to put in the hard graft to make it all happen on the ground level should not be ignored or overlooked.

And this is how you need to approach all of these situations. You need to make every decision from the same standpoint you made it when you were in operations. Remember back to a previous chapter when we looked at how you consider the skills and attitudes of your team before delivering a change? Well, guess what?

You still need to take this approach. The right way to do things hasn't changed just because you have a more expensive suit and a bigger car. But you can't speak to every individual involved in a decision. You can't deliver all the news yourself, or have those great conversations with colleagues and customers that you know cemented a positive change in the past. And that is why you have brought people along with you on the journey. You have generated a set of great people around you that believe in the same things you do. You have worked together for a long time and you all understand what is expected. It is still and will always be about, "People first and mission always." You can look at strategic decisions and immediately work out the tactical and operational challenges that these might mean. You have got to a place with your skills, your mindset and your team where you can ask all the relevant questions. What are the real strengths of the team? How can the individuals contribute to the team, department, division, organization and industries they touch? What does this mean to the outcomes we want? How long will it take to deliver excellence? The groups of people you have got together know what you want from them and how to deliver it. They have worked with you long enough to understand that ordinary just doesn't cut it. You need so much more than that.

You should begin to move them to the tip of their comfort zone. For some you will need to prove to them that the world is round and they will not fall off if they take one step forward. Others, you will need to acknowledge they are all they can be. The team you build around you will look at the challenges you set for exactly what they are – a challenge. The best environment to work in is one of high challenge and high support. This means that you set the bar really high but you give all the support that your team needs to meet those high challenges. Support can come in many ways, from a higher budget, to an investment in technology and also through positive messages. Support can mean different things to different people. The environment of high support and high challenge means that your team wants to do better each and every time. For example, if your target for this year is to launch 5 new products then next year they won't settle for anything less than 6. You have shaped people to think like you and work like you so why would you expect them to do anything other than challenge themselves like you? The quality of individuals that you surround yourself with determines the way that they work and the direction of the company. You have to think about who these people are and how they have come to work with you in the first place. Many will have come up through the ranks with you and been successful with you for a long time. Others will have migrated from other parts of the business to be a part of your team. Others still will have come from outside the company and may have been drawn to your team by YOU. Your influence and connections will bring highly motivated and top quality individuals towards you. The sphere of influence you have only grows as time goes by.

For a very select few, you will need to help them find their new paths of success and comfort. You have developed a working relationship with all of these people but it is so much more than that. You have developed a bond with all of your team that will last a lifetime. The great leader cultivates followers that will always be there when needed. And the effect works both ways. You will be surprised by the number of calls or emails you get from people who used to work for you. They want your advice, your support or your influence to help them resolve something. And because of the type of leader you are then you are always willing to give some of yourself to help one of your flock. This really is a bond for life. For some, their path may not be the same as yours. Even though they have been a valuable contributor to your success as a team there may always be a time where you have to part ways. Be the leader that you always have been and give support and your time to those that need your help in finding their true path.

Yes, you NOW carry their crosses so therefore don't marginalize hurt or have them ever go home thinking that they have let their families down. These are folks that go home to their spouses & children and are looked at as heroes. Their children want to emulate them when they grow up. You must be the empathic leader that considers the feelings and situations of each and every member of your team. Every one of us has thousands of things going on outside of the workplace and although the work we do together is vastly important in its own context, it my pale into insignificance compared to what is happening at home. Be the leader that cares. Be the leader that understands the human side of the business you are working in. By knowing your people from start to finish you have risen to your elevated level at the top of the pyramid so never stop being that person.

DO NOT EVER discount that your words don't just end careers; they tarnish souls and can crumble any confidence that they have. The power and influence you have can be a conduit for pain and distress as well as all the good things you want it to be about. Don't forget that you have a great deal of power behind the words you utter. As you are using your influence to secure contracts, do deals and move the company forward then influence is a positive thing. But the impact of the words that you may utter to your friends in a bar can have quite different impact on those that work in your organization. They say that actions speak louder than words but the higher up the organizational pyramid you are, the louder your words become. The whole company is looking to you for leadership and direction and the way you most often show that is by the communication you have with them. Keep this positive, keep this professional and see the rewards that you get. Just a positive word from someone of your level and standing can boost the confidence of one of your team immensely. The result is that you see a better level of work from them. This is seen as a small thing to many but to the person receiving the complement, it is massive. Take the time to speak to people. They will respond positively. Are you beginning to realize this three level chessboard is far more complex not just intellectually but emotionally demanding as well? (We will touch on the famous word Emotional Intelligence in a later chapter.) The game changes in many ways as you move up the levels. You have stopped just playing the pieces on the board and you now have to consider their emotions, their family life and the way that they respond. This just makes the game more interesting and actually adds a personal level to it all. As in previous chapters when we have looked at the different dimensions of the game as you move up the levels, you should never be scared to make a decision. Just because you now know that your words can make a huge impact it doesn't mean that you no longer speak to people. You will make your decisions and enact them based on the thought processes you have always used. This means that you can play the game of three-dimensional chess freely because you have the skills to succeed at the game. You are just playing the game on a bigger board with more pieces. But you are also playing the game with a bigger support team around you and much more experience than you had at the start.

You wanted to play at this level of chess and now you are the captain of not just your ship but theirs as well. This is an important consideration in everything that you do. At the start of this journey you probably thought about getting to the top in terms of what it meant for you. But you now have to think about what it means for everyone else. They have bought into your ethos and have traveled with you so far. You are the captain of many ships, all headed in the same direction. How you use your influence to guide these ships will determine the success of the sail. Be the leader that takes into account each and every one of your fellow travelers. Remember that you are all in this together.

EMPATHETIC LEADER

As you have progressed through the different levels of the board you will find that the style you operate under is successful. When you know the way to play the game of chess then this makes your style touch people in a certain way. The fact that you consider the actions and decisions you make in terms of the impact they have on others makes you an empathetic leader. You know the way that your decisions will be received and acted upon. You know the consequences on everyone in your organization and your customers. You know that to make the best decisions for all concerned you need to look at what it means to people. And that is the key difference between you and those other managers that don't quite have it. Instead of looking at each decision in terms of what it does to the balance sheet of the company, you are able to look at what it does to the balance sheet of the motivation and happiness of all concerned. You can separate a good business decision from a great decision for all of the business. The distinction may not even be on the radar of some others that you work with but for you it makes the job interesting – in fact it makes the job personal. Personality means a lot when it comes to working with others. The alternative would be a lone worker that doesn't have anyone else to bounce off. You will want to surround yourself with personalities every day of your working life because this is what makes you tick. That is where the empathetic leader starts on their journey. That is how you have got to this level today.

Are you comfortable in your skin yet? Do you realize what your role is? Good...

I am pretty sure by now you are gaining comfort in your new skin, your new suit. It might feel at the moment that it is a bit large on you but really don't sweat it – you will fill it very soon. You can hear the message within the message. It is in everything that you do. You have become this "man of the people" by doing the right things. The three-dimensional chess game doesn't play itself. You have become a grand master and your every move is awaited with anticipation from many people in and around you. You see the story shared with you from heart to heart. You are no longer just listening but hearing. The team is beginning to believe in your commitment, one olive branch at a time. As you meet new people and they realize what you do (in some cases what you can do for them) then you build up this network of contacts. Just having the contact details of someone means nothing. When they associate it with the strength of your personality, the quality of your work and the depth of your heart then this turns a name on a page into something far more powerful and engaging. You become the person that people want to deal with. You become the person who solves problems. You become the person that everyone wants to know. And all of this happens because you know how to play the game properly and you consider the impact on others. It can really be that simple. Keep your feelers out there and keep your contacts primed. When you are making strategic decisions then you want to know what this means on the tactical and operational levels. You want to see those bottom levels of the chessboard. You want to know what effect this change will have on all those that have to implement it. Your decisions mean actions for others. Never underestimate the power of your words, your decisions and your actions. They resonate through the company in a way that perhaps only you can understand. You have worked your way through the levels so you can still remember the days when you had to respond to similar decisions. You know what it feels like to have to turn these into solutions. Put yourself in their shoes. It perhaps wasn't that long ago that you actually were in their shoes.

Don't think though that any of this is going to be a walk in the park. Being a success takes a lot of hard work and discipline. If it were just about turning up day after day, week after week, month after month and year after year then your organization would be full of successes. But it isn't. There are success stories but these will be people like you that have learned to play the game. They operate in a similar manner to you. You can forge alliances with these guys and know that you will be looked after. The tough road is going to be ahead of you and at some point you will go into a various number of transitions. You will face many "firsts" during this time and you have to approach each one with an open mind and an open heart - your first, debate, your first crisis, your first win and yes, your first, "Aha! Moment." The, "Aha!" moment is not just for you but also for the person you are engaged in discussion with. The moment is the point that each of you might say "Aha!" in your head. It is when everything clicks and you both realize that this is the person I've been looking for. They will begin to realize you really are the leader they have been looking for. This is the person that thinks the way that I do. This is someone I am going to see a lot of in my career. This is the one that is committed not just to the mission but to the people first and foremost. And that is what makes you different. You are the empathetic leader that looks at decision in terms of personal impact rather than what it adds to the bottom line. So in the short term a cut in expenditure or not replacing someone who has left can be seen as a good thing. It saves cost and reduces the balance sheet in the expenditure column. You may pat yourself on the back and think that you have saved a bit of money for the shareholders. And in the short term you may just be right.

But when you are plating there dimensional chess you see all of this differently. It is not about the single dimension of a little cost saving. It is the impact that saving this cost has on everyone else in that department. It is the consequences to customers who may jump ship and go to one of your rivals. It is the way it makes the rest of the team feel if there is a vacancy that is not going to be filled. They become fearful that they end up with extra workload, they may start looking elsewhere. But you are the grand master when it comes to playing this game. You have a tight grip on the reality of the situation. You have contacts set up well enough to know the way that people will feel about this and you make the decision that works. You are playing the long-term game. Nobody wins at chess after one move. You may make a single move and feel really good about the direction it is taking you but you know you haven't won. Then multiply this by the massive number of possibilities on the three dimensional chessboard and you can see how it just has to be a long-term game. You can't possibly make a winning move on your first turn at the board. Think about all of your moves in this way and you will see that the strategy of making the right moves for everyone is the one that has got you to the higher levels of the pyramid and is the strategy that will keep you here for a very long time. Becoming the empathetic leader is one thing. You start working with people on an operational level and you soon find that it is easy to consider the feelings of others. You go to work with an open heart and you find that your positivity draws others towards you. Operations are somewhere that people all pull together and you become so successful at it that you get that promotion. Your ability to be empathetic has got you on to the next rung of the ladder. When you get to be making the tactical decisions there is a little more competition. You will be working alongside people that have been here for some time and they give off the impression that they know all there is to know. But you still have the connections in the operational team and you can still be that empathetic leader because you can have those conversations that make a difference. You have the time to speak to everyone and spread your message of inclusion and positivity. This means that you are able to extend the great work you did in operations and can move up to the strategic level. Here it can be much more difficult to maintain the empathetic style. You are more detached from your customers and those in your organization that work directly with them. You spend less time with those people and more time in meetings or planning out the strategy of the company for the next 3 years, the next 5 years, the next 10 years and beyond. This is the time that you most need to be the empathetic leader. You have built up a team around you that have worked well for you because of the style and character that you have displayed in the past. This is not the time to abandon that character and abandon the team because you feel that you should become something else. Empathy is the most valuable quality that you have and you must realize the part it has played in getting you to where you are today. Embrace it. Make plans to keep using it. Get your team and network set up in the right way so that you can make decisions in an empathetic way. Remember as I have said before – you need to see all the levels of the three-dimensional chessboard. If you can't see what it going on there then you simply can't make the right decision for these people. They say true leaders commit to carrying others crosses as a badge of honor. I believe that to be true. I see that small win coming through action every day and those are the incremental victories that need to be celebrated daily when possible. This is all a part of becoming a great leader. You generate loyalty from people because your actions have their best interests at heart. You gain followers because you have done the right things. But along with this following and loyalty you also generate a responsibility at the same time. You stop carrying just your own cross but the crosses of all your followers as well. They rely on you to take them to the next level, the next success and the next pay rise. Their happiness at work and their dedication to your cause is now shaped by the decisions you make in which direction to steer the company in. You are the leader of not only their employment but their hopes and dreams too. They want you to succeed because they believe in you and all the things that you stand for. They want you to succeed because you have touched their work life in a positive way with your empathy. But they also want you to succeed for all the benefits that your success brings them. It makes their job more secure. It increases their pay packet and bonus. It makes them happier at work. It even makes them happier at home. You have the power to influence a lot of lives from your employees to their families and through to your customers. This is quite a responsibility that you have made for yourself and one that you should not take lightly. You should be proud of your team and all the things that you have achieved together. It is by working together that you have got to this place. Don't stop now. It is an honor to be able to carry the crosses of others. It becomes an honor because you have reached this position through looking after people with your decisions and actions. You have gotten this privileged place through empathy and you should thank this character trait that you have for allowing you to meet these people that you call your team.

PEACOCK TO FEATHER DUSTER

Don't ever think that you have "made it" and can sit back on what you have done. The time to look back is when your career is over and you are enjoying your retirement. While you are still working, the three-dimensional game of chess is still being played at all levels. There is a great deal of enjoyment to be had from playing the game and being a part of something successful. The organization you are working in and leading will be only as successful as your last move. Decisions and actions you made a long time ago are great to remember but don't often affect what you find right in front of you today. You have built up a level of influence and power within the organization and industry you work in but this means nothing if you don't make the most of it.

Always remember that the way you have played the game of three-dimensional chess to get you where you are now is still the way to play the game every day. The decisions you are making today will be judged in the near future, whereas judgment on what you have done in the past has already been and gone. You will get a very short space of time to celebrate the success that you and your team have delivered before it is on to the next thing. You have a company to run, customers to please and jobs to protect. Your team has come to depend on you to deliver constant success and this is no time to let them down. One of the most famous statements I have ever heard made to me was this one, "I watched him go from Peacock to feather duster in 5 minutes". I remember this silver haired, seasoned executive who was wearing the traditional gray suit at the time, with a white shirt and blue conservative tie, as if he were still standing in front of me. He had his coffee mug in his hand shaking his head as he spoke that unforgettable phrase. He was referring to a meeting in a boardroom that had taken place. He referred to it as the beginning of the end for this one peer of his. I quickly learned it was the end in most cases. The time you have at the top may be fleeting for any one of a number of factors. You may find that you cross too many members of the board with the style you have – even though it is successful it may not be to their taste. You may find that it is time to go and work with another company or even in another industry. However long the time is you have at the top it will come to an end one day. You may well be the person who goes from peacock to feather duster. It can happen to us all.

I read this morning an article about an individual who was fired by what the writer was depicting as a bad manager, a new manager to his organization. He had put manager in quotes, whenever he referenced this alleged bad manager. I think it took away from the article but I believe the point was simple, "poor leaders in positions of power can independently and willfully destroy not only careers but companies". When I began to think through it, I could not but ask myself what did the writer and those that felt as strongly as he did do to course correct this alleged wrong done unto to this great employee? What were they willing to do to save their "peacock"? Great leaders will generate a great sphere of influence.

Although they may not be liked at board level, if they have come up through the ranks and built the right network of relationships then they will have a following. It is like the modern influence of social media. When a celebrity or entrepreneur creates a large and loyal following on Twitter, for example, then their views hold a lot of weight. Their followers will support their views and help them to defend against attacks from others. This will be the same with you and the team of loyal supporters you have gained. As you play the game of three-dimensional chess in the right way and get more people on your side then it can be more difficult for those in power to remove you.

I believe good people gravitate to one another; they go to the proverbial battle for their supervisors and their team members not necessarily the company. This is one of the reasons why you tend to see a flush out of departments or companies when one great leader heads over to another company then the rest of the team follow. They see the opportunities that their leader has created and want more of that. They feel valued by their leader and want to continue to feel like that. They see their career moving in an upward direction quickly and don't want to jeopardize that. The great leader generates a whole host of feelings in their team. They have been to the front together and won the fight. This in itself creates a feeling of camaraderie that is a very strong bond. The team that works well together to achieve challenging results in a happy and supportive environment wants to do this more and more every day. The team wants to be together because they know how each other works, they know how to motivate each other and they know how to succeed together. This is a very powerful connection that inspires people to come back to work day after day. This is when people look forward to getting out of bed and travelling to work. And all of this starts with a great leader and how they make their team feel. Once a great leader leaves their position, especially if they have worked for a company for some time, then you will find that the team tends to break apart and many will follow that leader. They follow their peacock. They follow the person that has been the catalyst for their career. They follow the person that has got them to the level they are at now. Organizations know all too well the cost of each employee. They know what the salary is for each member of their staff and they can see the figures printed on paper for their payroll. But what many organizations have not got a hold of are the intangibles that go along with this. The way that a great leader makes people feel is a huge intangible that makes an equally huge difference to work rates, employee retention and efficiency. It may be incredibly difficult to measure but when a great leader leaves the void that they leave behind is much easier to spot. You will see levels of morale drop, employees more likely to leave and productivity takes a dive. These are very real issues that any organization needs to consider when they look at losing a peacock. On the opposite end, I have experienced that as some great managers step into senior positions, they allow the golden handcuffs to guide their decisions. They may now concern themselves with the size of their paycheck, bonus, company car, golf membership and gym perks and all the other things that make their life a little easier. It appears that they had forgotten about the spitfire persona, leadership skills, high level of competency and ability to hear with their ears and listen with their hearts that got them to where they are today. This is a real shame when this happens and can lead to a stay in the boardroom being a short lived one. It was by playing the game of three-dimensional chess successfully with heart and empathy that got you here. Why would you even consider leaving it behind now? Those traits that allowed them to shine or be seen as great colorful peacocks are mothballed and placed on a mantle for their nostalgic moments. The equity they had built in loyalty currency where the team, teams and armies of people that would bang on the hammers of hell for them at a moment's notice, are now a distant memory. Don't let those glories of the past fade into the past. You should be making decisions today that will deliver the next glory and the one after that. You are a great leader and have proven this time after time. The day that you decide to sit back and look upon all of this as just a way to make more money is the day that you start to slip. Your team will notice, your customers will notice and your results will slide as well. Don't decide that your day is over because all of your influence will go to waste. All that goodwill and network that you built up through doing the right things by people every time will evaporate. You will work with many leaders like yourself over your career. Some will be playing the same game as you and you will naturally gravitate towards them. You may well be a part of a long succession line of leader after leader that has treated people in the right way to achieve success. As we have seen right throughout this book you get real, organic and inclusive success by looking at each decision based on the impact it has on others. The people above and below you in the organizational pyramid can be the easiest to see but there are others to think about too. You have people on different levels of the three dimensional chessboard and you need to be able to think about the consequences to them of your actions with every move. The customers at the end of the line are the lifeblood that determines how well your company performs. If they are not considered as the most important part of every single decision and action then the company is likely to fail. You have had to play the game in just the right way to get to where you are today. I have worked with many leaders throughout my time in business. You can learn how not to do things from the bad leaders you encounter. It is much more fun, however to work with the great leaders. There have been some bad ones. I will share that I have been lucky to work for great ones as well. These peacocks shaped our culture as a team. They were quick to deflect accolades with such a high level of humility that you learned from it. They were fair and firm but knew when to celebrate those incremental victories that were needed to galvanize the teams' overall achievements and positioned them well within the organization. This is the way to view your team's success. It is great to acknowledge and celebrate a success today but tomorrow it all starts again. You have new markets to reach, new customers to excite and engage. There are sales to make and questions to be answered. You have to plan for the next day, the next week, the next month and the next year. And all of this fits into the framework of the long term strategic plans that you have shaped for your organization. Great leaders of the past have helped me to realize all of this. They knew it was OK to laugh loudly and join in on the fun. It was great to hear them consistently say, "please, thank you and good morning," because they wanted to and not because they had to.

And this is the lesson in itself. This sums up everything that we have been looking at. A great leader does all of this because they want to. They are not obliged under their contract to consider every member of their team in their plans and decisions. They do it because they want to. They are not compelled to build a network so they can stay in touch with the ground level. They do it because they want to.

I can't speak on the tangibility of the phrase shared with me some 20 years back but can assure you that every team wants a leader with foresight, vision, empathy, competency and presence. I want all of you to aspire to be a leader like this. I want this book to empower you all to go on to great things. I want you all to have enjoyed reading this as much as I have enjoyed writing it. Aspire to achieve greatness and remember all the while that the way to do this is to take people with you and not leave them behind. As you develop a style that is inclusive then you will generate a band of merry followers. To them, you will be their peacock.

I have always been a fan of that fancy bird and hope some of you are as well.

IT HAS BEEN MY PRIVILIDGE TO SERVE YOU

I hope this book helps you see and know that good guys don't finish last, that doing what is right when no one is watching is a great thing, that hearing with your ears and listening with your heart does work and that sharing your heart with your extended family, your work family is OK. This whole book has been about sharing. I have travelled a similar path to the one you are on and let me tell you it is amazing. You get to spend your day working with fantastic people in a caring environment. By playing the game of three-dimensional chess in a considerate way you cultivate relationships and friendships that last a lifetime. Remember every player on every level of the board whenever you make a move and you will see that two things occur. The first is that you become a success. The second is that others gravitate towards you. The way that you treat other people is remembered.

Leadership is a privilege and not an entitlement so cherish your time leading great people, departments of companies, as they all need good ones. You will start to find that like-minded people are drawn to you. As you sit there and look at your team you know what they are capable of. You know how to motivate them to greater things. Remember the environment of high challenge and high support because this is what gets the best out of each and every one of them. You spend a lot of your life at work so to do it in the presence of great people makes it all the better. As a leader you are responsible for the hopes and dreams of your whole team. You carry all their crosses so make every day enjoyable and make every decision inclusive.

Via this book and these words it has been my privilege to serve you and I hope to read about all of you great peacocks over time. I hope that some of my wisdom and experience passes through these pages to you. It has been a pleasure to impart this information to you and I hope that you get some confidence and knowledge from the words I have put together here. I want you all to be great leaders and enjoy the challenges and emotions that this brings.

I look forward to being one of your biggest fans. I look forward to reading about your success. I look forward to seeing happy teams all over the world that are inspired to come to work every day by the great leader you have become. Always remember the three-dimensional chess board because it runs through everything you do. Every decision you make needs to take into account the people that it affects. It sounds so simple when put in these terms but it is the most often overlooked part of management. As you have risen through the ranks from making operational decisions, through the time of tactical decision making to the top of the pyramid and the strategic decisions you will have made it there by considering the impact of your decisions. The people that work in your organization are the ones that turn those plans and decisions into realities for themselves and the customers that your company serves. Make it as easy as possible for those teams to deliver excellent results and they will back you all the way.

It has been my pleasure and privilege to serve you.

Your soon to be biggest fan,

Maurizio

Area to reflect on YOUR journey

_____
_____
_____
_____
_____
_____
_____
_____
_____
_____
_____
_____
_____
_____
_____
_____
_____
_____
_____
_____
_____
_____
_____
_____
_____
_____
_____
_____
_____

Made in the USA
Lexington, KY
27 May 2018